Writing Doctoral Project Proposals:

Higher Education Research

(Second edition 2015)

Prof Paul Trowler

About this book

This book is designed to be as helpful as possible for anyone who needs to write a doctoral research proposal in the area of higher education research. It is concise, while still being comprehensive and useful. Its audience is prospective doctoral students who have to write a project proposal which will be assessed for admission and perhaps for a scholarship to do their doctoral research, as well as those who have already been admitted to university but now need to have a full proposal approved.

For readability, terms which may need a fuller explanation are linked from the text to a glossary at the end of the book. Terms in the text that are described in the glossary are printed in bold.

This second edition adds new material and offers examples of proposals for doctoral research projects together with a commentary on them suggesting improvements. The aim is to help the reader develop an 'eye' for a persuasive argument and a good feel for a well-integrated proposal.

Contents

Introduction

Applicants for a doctoral degree and those already on a doctoral programme normally have to supply a project proposal as part of their application. For initial applicants this is one of the three ways in which universities normally make selection decisions. These three ways involve asking and answering these questions:

1. Is the applicant sufficiently qualified and capable to do a doctorate (as judged by their CV and track record)?

2. Is the research project proposal of high enough quality, practicable and important enough to be acceptable (as judged by the written proposal and perhaps a defence of it in interview)?

3. Is there a supervisor who is able and willing to supervise the proposal?

Each university's requirements regarding the research project proposal (point 2) are slightly different, but for the Department of Educational Research at Lancaster University the requirement is a fairly standard one: doctoral project proposals should be up to 1,000 words and should cover the following areas:

Title of the Research: A meaningful, provisional title that summarises the area of interest and planned programme of research. There should be a central problematic in the title, not simply a description of the field to be studied.

Research Questions: Identification of the main research question(s) being asked. These should be succinct, researchable and significant. Bullet points are usually best.

Background to the Research Topic: Explanation of how the questions are different from those asked by others, drawing on a brief review of the relevant research literature. This should show familiarity with the main literature in the field of interest.

Research Design & Methods: The 'who', 'what', 'where' and 'why' of the research plan. There should be an explanation of how the method(s) used will answer the research questions.

Significance of the Research: The contribution that this research will make. Identify the implications of the research for existing educational theories, policy or practice in higher education.

Research Timetable: A detailed timetable that shows how the research design can be managed within a three year time period (or a 5 year period for part time students).

Bibliography: The main written sources on which the research will be based.

The rest of this short book is organized with this structure at its core. At the end of the book are two chapters outlining the more creative aspects of the process of deciding on a topic and developing a proposal.

Title of the Project

The title of the proposed project is important because it sums up the focus and significance of the envisaged research. A good title should make it clear what the central problematic is, the key issue being addressed. This should be done succinctly and perhaps might even indicate the research design being used.

However many authors of doctoral proposals fail to do this and instead make one of the following three mistakes:

* Using verbs like 'explore' or 'investigate': these are too open-ended. For example: *"Exploring Teleconferencing in Further Education in the UK"*. This indicates vagueness in the mind of the candidate and the potential danger of an endless doctorate, because there are no parameters or clear goals.

* Contrasting two possibilities and asking which is correct. For example *"Positive Change or 'Self-Righteous Waffle': Academics' Perspectives on Sustainability Policy in Universities."* This indicates simplistic binary thinking and suggests that 'straw men' are being set up to be easily knocked down

* Writing a sentence which is just descriptive and lacks a problematic. For example *"The Motivational Effect of Technical and Vocational Education on Students in India."* There is no issue evident: it is unclear what the project is specifically about.

Much better are titles which give an immediate feel for the key issue at hand, and even an indication of the research design:

"Can Students Influence Policy Implementation in Higher Education? : A Case Study Based on the Mainstreaming of Liberal Adult Education." (The title of a PhD by D.F.M. Butt, Reading University, 2000).

"A critical review of the role of the English funding body for higher education in the relationship between the State and higher education in the period 1945-2003". (The title of a PhD by D.J. Taggart, Bristol University, 2004).

Research Questions

Research questions should:
- Be answerable: it must be possible to know when a question has been answered
- Be specific, that is set clear boundaries in terms of what is being studied, and what is not
- Include at least one analytical question which goes beyond the descriptive
- Be capable of **operationalisation**; that is, use concepts that can be turned into measureable, observable, describable phenomena
- Be bounded in what they require, that is they can be realistically answered given the resources available
- Be significant; that is, they should provide an answer to the 'so what?' question - the issue of offering wider interest to a larger audience

One role of research questions is to guide research design, and there needs to be congruence between that design and the questions. This means that the research design chosen must be capable of answering the research questions.

Here is a problematic attempt at constructing research questions:

> This project aims to explore academic staff's reception of the teaching and learning policy of a university. The analysis will focus on the discourse that arises from staff's reaction to the policy as well as factors that could undermine or facilitate the achievement of the policy.

This is more like part of an abstract than research questions: while these statements give a feel for the proposed research, there is no specificity, only broad aims.

While they give licence to the writer to cover
seems interesting, they fail to set boundaries. It w
to the writer when their work has stepped outside
the study. The word 'explore' is particularly dang
respect - it does not set boundaries or specific goals.
'Reception' is capable of multiple interpretations and needs to
be operationalised. There are too many questions wrapped up
in these two sentences: they need to be unpicked.
Those two sentences could be reconfigured as follows:

> 1. To what extent do academic staff in one Faculty in a
> new university in the UK display knowledge about and
> understanding of the formal teaching and learning
> policy there?
> 2. In what different ways do academic staff there
> interpret and respond to that policy?
> 3. What reasons can be given for the differences
> identified in answering questions 1 and 2?
> 4. What different **discursive repertoires** do they draw on
> when they discuss the policy?
> 5. What are the implications of the answers to questions
> 1-4 for policy implementation in the area of teaching and
> learning in the case study university?
> 6. To what extent do these findings confirm what is
> known about policy implementation in that context?
> 7. What are the implications of the findings for
> university managers at senior and middle levels in that
> context?

These research questions, unpicked in this way, themselves
raise issues about the **truth claims** that can be made from a
study of one Faculty in one university, but recognising this as
an issue is enough for a project proposal.
Analysing these questions further:
Question 1 requires a fairly descriptive answer but there are
more analytical ones to follow.
Question 2 is possibly still too open, but it is an improvement
on the original version.

...estion 3 allows the writer to do some analysis which might get him or her into disciplinary differences, institutional location etc. The data collection needs to be thoughtfully constructed to be able to answer it, and a pilot study undertaken to ensure this.

Question 4 (based on the original version) stands out as possibly belonging to a different thesis, and being potentially too big, especially when Question 5 is attempted.

Question 6 allows a discussion of the literature and gives the thesis a theoretical edge.

Question 7 might be further refined, or possibly dropped if the thesis becomes too big - question 6 covers some of this already. It also begs the 'so what' question – why should anyone other than senior and middle managers in that institution be interested?

Because of question 6 the main answer to the 'so what' question appears to be a theoretical one in relation to the literature on policy implementation. That would be fine, and the applicant needs to make it clear that this is the main priority of the project, with other aims being significant but perhaps not central.

Often it is useful to distinguish between the **locus** and the **focus** of a doctoral proposal – a topic of study can be merely the location through which deeper questions are explored. In this case the locus is the teaching and learning policy in one Faculty in one university, but the focus is actually achieving a better understanding of the implementation of change. Research question 6 is the key one, if this approach were to be taken in this example.

Research Questions: The seven deadly sins

1. Too descriptive – *"What are the management styles in place in Saudi Arabian universities?"* (This is OK if there are more analytical questions after it, though of course it is ambitious).

2. Too narrow – *"How can the use of e-portfolios at the University of Bentham be improved?"* (Who cares – apart from people at Bentham?).

3. Too ambitious – *"What teaching and learning approaches are in place in UK higher education and how can they be improved?"* (Impossible to answer).

4. Only focused on perceptions – *"In what different ways do Accountancy lecturers at the University of Bentham view the merger of their Department with the Department of Statistics there?"* (**So what**?).

5. Too vague – *"How does the higher education system in Chile differ from that in Argentina"?* (How long have you got?).

6. **Normative** – *"What are the benefits of linking research and teaching in universities?"* (What about the dysfunctions?).

7. Too **prescriptive** – *"Why does the modular system in UK higher education need to be changed?"* (Predicts the outcome without actually doing the research).

Note how the deadly sins are rarely found alone – problematic questions often combine two or more.

Background to the Research Topic

This section of a research project proposal should set out the context to the issue for research: this will definitely include the relevant literature but (depending on the topic) might also include the policy background, the contemporary relevance of the topic or some other background factors that are relevant.

The aim of the section is to demonstrate a reasonable knowledge of the area (recognising of course that the research hasn't been done yet), to situate the issue for the panel assessing the application, to show why the proposed research is important, and to show what the research could offer that is significant.

The section should not be too long: often candidates assume that a very extended discussion of the literature will impress. Of course to some extent it does, especially when that discussion shows the ability to evaluate research critically. However, more impressive is the thinking behind the description of the proposed research itself when this demonstrates clarity in conceptualising a very concrete, doable and clearly envisaged research design, the outcomes of which will advance knowledge in some way. So the background section needs to be kept fairly brief, and the discussion of the literature oriented to showing where there are deficiencies or gaps that will be addressed by the research.

It is important not to simply take descriptive content straight from websites or other sources. Apart from the potential issue of plagiarism, that content is unlikely to be oriented to the proposed topic of research. It is really important that all aspects of the background section are situated in relation to the specifics of the proposed research. Too often in doctoral proposals descriptive material is dissociated from any attempt to demonstrate its significance.

Research Design & Methods

This is probably the hardest part of writing a research proposal, and is often very significant in terms of whether the whole proposal is convincing or not. Clearly, once enrolled, the candidate's supervisor will help him or her to develop a good research design. But it is necessary to make a convincing attempt at it in the research proposal.

Sometimes candidates fall back on **grounded theory** in developing their proposals: basically arguing that they will collect the data and see what comes out of them. However this often fails to convince selection panels and in general it is better to set out a clear, convincing, planned research design. The key thing in this is to make sure that the design chosen is capable of answering the research questions; indeed is the *best* way to answer the research questions.

In general the research design should make clear:

- what the units of analysis are (institutions, departments, people);
- which (or which types of these) of these will be selected for data collection, how many and why;
- what type of data collection methods will be used, and why;
- how the data will be analysed.

Often, a diagram can sum up the descriptive elements of the above more clearly and succinctly than can a written description. But of course the rationale for the design needs to be elaborated in writing.

Ethical issues need to be addressed, as do questions of access: it is often harder to secure agreement to participate than is at first imagined, even for insider researchers: simply assuming that the data will be easily obtainable is not convincing, but thinking ahead about this at least demonstrates awareness of the issue.

Questions and answers

The key issue in research design is ensuring that the decisions made are guided by the research questions: the data generated by the research must be appropriate and sufficient to provide robust answers to the questions asked. It is also important to ensure that a consistent and defensible approach is taken towards **epistemological** and **ontological** issues: what does the research claim can be known about the social reality under investigation and how is that reality conceived?

A **realist** ontological position will usually mean more positivist research designs utilising predominantly quantitative data generation approaches which yield statements describing correlations of a generalisable nature. On the other hand a social constructionist position is likely to be more qualitatively inclined and quite limited in its claims for generalisability.

There are many excellent textbooks on research design, data collection and the role of theory. Here I concentrate on the key issues of relevance to insider researchers.

The following section on research design and methods is drawn from my book on **Insider Research in Universities**, aimed at those researching or planning to research the institution in which they are employed or are currently a student. For more information on this area, including 'outsider' research, see the latest edition of Judith Bell's book *Doing Your Research Project*.

Single and multi-site studies

Insider researchers are usually faced with multiple pressures on their time and limited resources to use in the research. Some will be employed by the university and have more financial resources but limited time for the research, others will be full-time students studying their own university, with more time but less cash. In either case the option of doing a single-site case study is attractive for practical reasons, and as the next chapter shows can be valuable in itself. Coleman and von Hellermann (2011) and their contributors advocate doing ethnographic studies based on anthropological methods conducted on the researcher's own 'turf':

> ...the 'field' has traditionally been conceptualized as being 'out there' (away from the anthropologist's home), enclosed within a definable territory, and best understood through the method of participant observation. Bound up with these practices is the assumption that culture is located 'out there', with ethnography being about the unfamiliar 'other'. Participant observation traditionally involves intensive dwelling and interaction with the 'native' in order to understand his or her worldview...Such positing of people, places, and 'culture' is increasingly critiqued on account of the problematic ideological assumptions..."
> (Mand, 2011: 42)

These assumptions include the notion that 'culture' is something exotic and 'other', amenable only to the distanced and more analytical academic eye, eventually represented through the godlike authorial voice. Insider research which views the local and familiar is at least as valuable, they argue.

But as well as seeing the value of single-site insider research, Coleman and von Hellermann explore the problems and possibilities of *multi*-site ethnographies including those conducted 'at home'. However, as Marcus acknowledges (p. 27, in Coleman and von Hellerman), attempting to deploy such a labour-intensive method of data collection as ethnography in multiple sites will "overwhelm the norms of intensive, patient work in ethnography".

For the individual researcher such a design is too ambitious. This means that a multi-site approach which uses mixed methods or less labour-intensive methods than ethnography may have benefits which justify their costs in terms of time and labour. The important issue in making decisions around this is appropriateness in terms of the research questions, which themselves then come into the mix of factors to consider when planning research which is both practicable and valuable.

For the insider researcher developing a project which compares results from their own institution to those elsewhere, a multi-site study is obviously the way to go - unless other studies have already been conducted elsewhere which are close enough to their own.

Examples of such comparative projects include:

    1. The factors influencing the success or otherwise of an innovation

    2. Approaches to management and leadership and their effectiveness

    3. The implementation of a national policy at ground level, including compliance (or otherwise) with national quality (or other) guidelines

    4. Professional practices in a discipline or field of study

    5. Student responses to an innovation

Action research

Bensimon et al (2004: 105) suggest that it is important for practitioners concerned with bringing about change in their context to "produce knowledge in local contexts to identify problems and take action to solve them". The authors in that collection advocate the idea that change agents should be 'practitioners-as-researchers'.

Action research is an emergent enquiry process involving cycles of: actions; enquiry, analysis; planning; changed actions. It has, broadly, an enhancement agenda. But there are ofen different understandings of what 'enhancement' may involve, especially among those on the ground in universities.

Action research can be undertaken with different audiences, beneficiaries and purposes in mind. It can be emancipatory in intent, aiming to identify disadvantaged groups and to rectify structural disadvantage, or it can simply be aimed at making sure policy is implemented effectively, regardless of what it is or its effects.

Useful guides to conducting action research are Coghlan and Brannick (2010) and Koshy (2009).

Evaluative research

Evaluative research in higher education aims to attribute value and worth to individual, group, institutional or sectoral activities happening there (Saunders, Trowler and Bamber, 2011). Because this guide concentrates on insider research, the relevant levels of evaluative activity are the individual, group and university ones. Such research asks questions about the value of long-standing activities or of innovations that the researcher is undertaking, or those of a group to which s/he belongs, or those of the university as a whole.

While evaluative research often deploys similar data generation techniques to those of 'regular' research, and can use theory in similar ways too, there is one key question presented by this kind of research if it is to be lifted beyond the particular. That is – 'what is the value of this in terms of a larger contribution to knowledge in the academic world?' If the research focuses on the value of a particular set of activities, or an innovation, in a particular location at a particular time, then it becomes difficult to answer that question. Furthermore, the chances of getting a study of a particular situation published in a reputable journal are rather small, if that is an aim of the research.

There are three key ways in which evaluative studies can be conducted so that they provide good answers to this 'contribution' question and stand a good chance of being published, at least in part. These are: *theoretical* contribution; *methodological* contribution; *professional* contribution. Often good evaluative studies will offer a combination of these.

The *theoretical* contribution relates to some aspect of the relevant literature, perhaps on implementation theory or the management of change, or some aspect of theory related to the substance of the activity or innovation (information and communication technologies, for example). The later part of this chapter deals with the place of theory in research.

The *methodological* contribution relates to evaluative methodology, the techniques and theories employed in conducting evaluative research, and the study should offer something additional to what already exists in this area.

There are a number of different approaches to evaluative research, methodologically and in other ways, so the contribution can be made to one or more of these.

In summary they are: technical-rational evaluation; appreciative enquiry (**Cooperrider and Srivastva**, 1987); utilization-focused evaluation (Patton, 1997) and finally realistic evaluation (Pawson and Tilley, 1997). An overview of these is offered in chapter 2 of Saunders, Trowler and Bamber, 2011.

Finally, the *professional* contribution relates to practice in the area being investigated, and to achieve this it is necessary to expand the truth claims of the research beyond simply establishing the value of the particular activity or innovation to encompass *similar* activities/innovations in similar circumstances. In this third category the issues covered in the next chapter become particularly relevant.

Institutional ethnography

This is an approach to researching what its founder, Dorothy Smith (2005; 2006), describes as the "textually-mediated social organization". Smith says that institutional ethnography begins by locating a standpoint within an institutional order, a particular guiding perspective from which to explore that order.

This raises a set of concerns, issues or problem germane to those people who occupy that standpoint. These "local actualities of the everyday world" (Smith, 2005: 34) are only the starting point however. From here the investigation of institutional processes is launched, and the broader structural forces which impinge on the everyday world are explored.

Because of this unfolding from the local it is not always possible to sketch a detailed research design in advance. But Smith argues that the design is not random: "Each next step builds from what has been discovered and invades more extended dimensions of the institutional regime" (2005: 35). Language, and textual objects are very significant in this – for Smith language serves to co-ordinate subjectivities.

Devault (2006: 294) says this:

> Institutional ethnographies are built from the examination of work processes and study of how they are coordinated, typically through texts and discourses of various sorts. Work activities are taken as the fundamental grounding of social life, and an institutional ethnography generally takes some particular experience (and associated work processes) as a "point of entry." The work involved could be part of a paid job; it might fall into the broader field of unpaid or invisible work, as so much of women's work does; or it might comprise the activities of some "client" group.

This examination is conducted through the standard mix of ethnographic approaches; interviews, observation, documentary analysis and so on. But careful attention is paid in particular to the use of textual artefacts, the discursive repertoires employed in them and the causes of effects of these on social relations within organizations.

In Smith's original formulation there is a concern to investigate the ruling relations that are articulated in work processes and instantiated in texts, and she pays particular attention to the ways in which women are subjugated within institutional processes and through texts and discourses.

For example in universities 'mothering work' can be a discursively and organizationally embedded in such a way that women academics disproportionately find themselves doing low-status and unrecognised work supporting students in difficulties.

And of course what in some contexts are called 'support staff' are disproportionately female in most universities.

How this has come to be, and how it is perpetuated, are areas that can usefully be explored in a fine-grained way through institutional ethnography. And not only explored. A key tenet of the approach is that it should be *for* people and not just *about* them: the research must illuminate the mechanisms of oppression and disadvantage and suggest ameliorative strategies.

Institutional ethnography sees local practices in terms of the larger picture of structured advantage and disadvantage, despite the fact that it starts from a particular standpoint within the institution. In this it addresses one of the criticisms sometimes made of fine-grained ethnographic research, for example by Hamersley (1993) and Porter (1993), that such research loses sight of the structural constraints on actors and structural conditioning of their behaviour.

It is clear that insider research and institutional ethnography are highly compatible, at least for some kinds of research questions.

However as an approach to enquiry it does leave the researcher with some problematic questions. One is: what standpoint should I start from and how do I draw the limits around it?

This is a question of level of analysis: the standpoint might be that of 'students', or 'women students', or 'women students with disabilities'.

That last category could itself be segmented further. Another question is: if I start from one standpoint and work outwards, as Smith recommends, what about other standpoints that exist in the university – why should I privilege just this one?

These and many other questions need good answers if readers are to be convinced that the study is robust.

Hypothesis testing

Here the purpose of insider research is to test an hypothesis or to replicate a previous study in a different but relevant context in order to test its conclusions. Either qualitative or quantitative approaches may be adopted to do this, or a combination of both.

This research purpose is best illustrated by an example. Such research could involve a study designed to test the hypothesis developed by Arum and Roksa (2011) that universities (at least in the USA) are "academically adrift". Arum and Roksa used the Collegiate Learning Assessment, a standardized test administered to students in their first semester and then again at the end of their second year, as well as survey responses to answer the question: "do students learn the important things that universities claim to deliver?" They conclude that 45 percent of the students included in their data demonstrate no significant improvement in critical thinking, complex reasoning, and writing during their first two years of college.

In addition Arum and Roksa extrapolate from their analysis some explanations: one is that students are distracted from their studies by socializing or by working at the same time. A further cause is the fact that universities and their staff prioritise other things than undergraduate learning, such as research. In addition there is, they claim, deliberate collusion between staff and students not to tax each other too much.

Methodologically this study has come under criticism, most notably from Alexander **Astin** (2011), and there are many claims in it that are unsubstantiated and which from a UK perspective appear to be just wrong (for example about the findings of the majority of studies on the 'teaching-research nexus').

So, this study could be tested in a different but relevant context. A similar or identical research design could be adopted to test the findings, and the same statistical techniques could be applied to the data. Alternatively the hypothesised causes of this claimed lack of significant learning could be explored. A further alternative is to build on Astin's critique and design a 'better' study.

Theory and insider research

Theory-use is very important in research generally and insider research in particular – it lifts it above mere market research or journalism, and it allows the researcher to step outside generally accepted ways of seeing the social world.
'Theory' is usually portrayed as consisting of six linked characteristics:

1. It uses a set of interconnected concepts to classify the components of a system and how they are related.

2. This set is deployed to develop a set of systematically and logically related propositions that depict some aspect of the operation of the world.

3. These claim to provide an explanation for a range of phenomena by illuminating causal connections.

4. Theory should provide predictions which reduce uncertainty about the outcome of a specific set of conditions. These may be rough probabilistic or fuzzy predictions, and they should be corrigible – it should be possible to disconfirm or jeopardize them through observations of the world. In the **hypothetico-deductive** tradition, from which this viewpoint comes, theory offers statements of the form 'in Z conditions, if X happens then Y will follow'.

5. Theory helps locate local social processes in wider structures, because it is these which lend predictability to the social world.

6. Finally, theory guides research interventions, helping to define research problems and appropriate research designs to investigate them.

Different levels and types of theory inform decisions, processes and outcomes in research (see Trowler, 2012, for an account of them).

There are also different views on the role of theory, some challenging its fundamental role, as set out above, and seeing it not as part of a 'scientific' process but as creative and emancipatory. Feminist thinkers, among others, tend to adopt this perspective:

> how often their own cherished analytical rationality is broken up by glimpses into the imagination of more provocative thinkers. I have come to the conclusion that it is not so much that we self-consciously assemble all the resources for the making of research imaginaries as those vivid ideas (and frequently their authors) come to haunt us. (Hey, 2006: 439)

Stephen Ball agrees:

> Theory is a vehicle for 'thinking otherwise', it is a platform for 'outrageous hypotheses' and for 'unleashing criticism'. Theory is destructive, disruptive and violent. It offers a language for challenge, and modes of thought, other than those articulated for us by dominant others. It provides a language of rigour and irony rather than contingency. The purpose of such theory is to de-familiarise present practices and categories, to make them seem less self-evident and necessary, and to open up spaces for the invention of new forms of experience. (Ball, 1995: 265-6)

Haraway (1991) takes this point further in elabora
notion of 'standpoint theory'. Sprague and Hayes, ..
discussing the concept, say this:

> Standpoint epistemology argues that all knowledge is
> constructed in a specific matrix of physical location,
> history, culture, and interests... A standpoint is not the
> spontaneous thinking of a person or a category of
> people. Rather, it is the combination of resources
> available in a specific context from which an
> understanding might be constructed. (Sprague and
> Hayes, 2000: 673).

For Sprague and Hayes, as for Smith (2005), discussed above,
it is important to challenge the standpoint of the privileged
from the standpoint of the disadvantaged and (as feminists)
from that of women. This can bring empowerment and self-
determination; it uses theory as a weapon against structures of
privilege and structured disadvantage.

> Feminist standpoint theory suggests that an important
> way to develop this line of research is to build on the
> standpoints of those who are least empowered in our
> current relationships. People living in different
> intersections of gender, class, and race are likely to have
> different stories to tell. Thus, a good way to start is to
> listen to people with disabilities who are also women
> and/or poor and/or people of color, and the people who
> nurture them, as they describe in their own ways the
> constraints on their daily lives... (Sprague and Hayes,
> 2000: 690).

Insider research presents particular problems in terms of the
use of theory and the relationship between theory and data.
 Insiders conducting emic research are themselves liable to be
influenced by tacit theories held by respondents.

They can even be captured by institutional or by management discourse, as Hammersley argues (see Trowler, 2001, for more on this).

In such cases it becomes particularly difficult to render the normal strange, to move beyond the standpoint of the privileged. But human behaviour viewed through the microscope tends to bring to attention impalpable drivers far more than when it is seen through a telescope and by their nature these are difficult to apprehend through pure empiricism. In fine-grained qualitative insider research knowledgeability and sense-making are foregrounded as explanation is prioritised above simple correlation. In this respect the role of theory in insider research holds both promise and dangers.

The seven deadly sins of research design

1. Not being specific enough about the details of the sample selected for study and the rationale for that selection.

2. Adopting a research design which is not appropriate to answering the research questions.

3. Not giving a rationale for the overall research design.

4. Proposing a 'convenience' sampling approach without acknowledging the consequences of this for the robustness of the study: being too complacent about what is acceptable.

5. Not explaining how the different components of the research design can be integrated during analysis – especially in a mixed-methods design.

6. Not acknowledging potential ethical issues.

7. Not giving a convincing answer to the '**so what**' question in terms of what the data can offer.

Significance of the Research

Doctoral research must demonstrate that a significant contribution has been made to knowledge in its field, and must at least in part be publishable in an academic journal.

While it might be presumptuous to identify so far in advance what that significant contribution will be, it is important to show that the research at least has the potential to jump this hurdle. Doubts about this might be raised in admission panel members' minds if the topic of the research appears to be too parochial; only concerned with the issues in one organization at a particular time, for example. These concerns may be magnified if the research design involves insider research. I deal with this in more detail in Chapter 4, *Value and Robustness*, of **Doing Insider Research in Universities**.

So in making it explicit why the research is important, and at a high enough level potentially to merit a doctorate, it is important to go beyond the particular. In discussing evaluative research in the previous chapter I identified some potential avenues for doing this. For other kinds of research alternative ways in which this can be done include:

- Testing, developing or elaborating a particular theoretical perspective or tradition
- Testing previous research findings in a new context
- Approaching questions previously addressed by other research using new methodological tools
- Developing conceptual models which illuminate some aspect of social reality
- Critiquing current positions in literature, policy or practice

- Building a basis for new policy or practice in wider contexts
- Developing new approaches to research
- Offering new insights into significant issues
- Bringing together and building on previous research findings

Research Timetable

The key point in setting out the research timetable is to be realistic. An over-ambitious timetable betrays lack of insight into the research process.

Time should be allocated at the beginning of the research for in-depth familiarisation with the literature and for refining the research design and questions as well as for developing data collection instruments. This almost always takes longer than expected: getting to grips with the literature will need to incorporate literature on relevant theory, on the substantive topic and on research methodology, so this alone is time-consuming.

It is important to conduct a pilot study (assuming the proposed research is empirically-based) before going into the field. Time needs to be allocated to this, and to processing the results from that pilot.

The time allocated to data collection and analysis depends, of course, on the research design, but again needs to be realistic. In most cases data analysis will occur concurrently with data generation rather than being a process left undone until after all the data have been 'collected'.

Writing up the thesis also takes longer than is sometimes imagined. A typical thesis will have six or seven chapters, and even with drafts of many of these already prepared, it can take between three and eight months of dedicated work to refine the whole thesis into a finished form. Setting out the structure of the thesis here can be helpful, serving to emphasise the clarity of the proposal. A fairly standard set of chapters looks like this:

1. Introduction
2. Contextualisation
3. Literature review
4. Method/ology
5. Data presentation and analysis
6. Conclusions

Different universities set different targets for their doctoral students, but the **Department of Educational Research** at Lancaster University sets the ones below. Such targets can act as a template for setting out the research timetable in a doctoral project proposal:

For Students in Year 1 (or Part-Time Equivalent):

- Research questions and research design finalised and agreed with supervisor.
- Good progress made with review of relevant literature.
- Scoping and pilot enquiries have validated research design in terms of potential of richness of data to answer questions.
- Key concepts and theoretical lens clear by end of year 1.

For Students in Year 2 (or Part-Time Equivalent):

- Data collection complete, or nearly so. Good progress on analysis.
- Some thesis chapters written in draft, including contextual-introductory chapters, methodology chapter, literature review.
- Good conceptualisation of probable findings and argument, including its engagement with the literature.
- Writing 'voice' for thesis now found.

For Students in Year 3 (or Part-Time Equivalent):

- Data analysis complete. Argument fully formed.
- Writing up full thesis.
- Presentations at conferences and departmental seminar to prepare for viva and improve structure of argument.
- Potential areas of discussion in viva identified

Writing a Bibliography

The key things in setting out the bibliography are: a) to set out in full the bibliographical details of any works cited in the proposal and b) to indicate other significant texts that will inform the project.

In doing this the panel assessing the project proposal will look for coverage of the field and for good practice in both citation and setting out a bibliography. Inconsistencies in how books and articles are referenced may be taken as a sign of poor research training or sloppiness in writing, and so should be avoided.

In research into higher education the usual citation and referencing conventions involve a version of the Harvard system. The style guide for authors from, for example, Open University press, is (in most cases) appropriate for a doctoral proposal for higher education research: **http://mcgraw-hill.co.uk/openup/authors.html**

Finding Inspiration

Often doctoral applicants and candidates have a firm view of the topic they want to research. This may be some issue that is important to them professionally, a puzzle that they want to spend time exploring great depth. It may have been suggested to them by a comment from a colleague, or by something they read. They may simply be continuing earlier studies but now within a much more focused and deeper doctoral framework. Turning this topic into a robust project proposal is the topic of the next chapter.

Sometimes though they do not have a very clear idea about what the topic of their doctoral research might be, or have two or three different ones and they are not sure which is the most viable.

In this latter case there are a number of ways of finding inspiration for researchable topics:

* Reading titles and abstracts of completed doctorates in the higher education field for areas that are of interest. Where there is access to the complete doctorate, looking for sections on 'further research' can be helpful. See ethos.bl.uk and http://www.theses.com/.

* Reflecting on what area of expertise they would like to be known for in four or five years' time, or what would be professionally most valuable.

* Reflecting on what kind of data collection methods would be most viable and interesting for them, and working back from that to a suitable topic.

* Reviewing topics currently being funded by relevant higher education research funding bodies such as (in the UK) the ESRC, HEA and LFHE.

* Investigating the website of preferred university departments to explore the research specialisms of likely supervisors.

* Reading books that give overviews of areas of research that are of interest with a view to exploring one of those areas further.

* Attending conferences and talking to people giving presentations on topics of interest about further research areas.

* Brainstorming and then progressively refining/combining ideas. See James Hayton's video on this: http://www.youtube.com/watch?v=PY01A-jCuOA&feature=player_embedded&CMP= .

(There are more resources about thesis writing from Hayton at http://3monththesis.com/)

From Sketchy Idea to Robust Project Proposal

STAGE	A Specific Example (for illustration only – a full proposal would have more)
Refine research questions	*"To what extent and to what ends can conceptions of 'learning organizations' as developed in management literature be applied in university contexts in the UK?"*
Develop research design appropriate for research questions	Review of management literature on 'learning organizations'. Secondary data from a varied sample of UK universities.
If necessary revisit research questions to establish better fit with research design	*"To what extent can models of 'learning organizations' as developed in management literature be used to establish how far UK universities fit those models, using secondary data?* *How far do those models need development for a UK university context, and what purposes would such a development serve?"*
Identify literature to be addressed	Management literature on 'learning organizations'.
Refine research design in a detailed way, especially in terms of sampling	15 UK universities will be sampled. Three will be selected from each of the 5 HE groupings in that country (Russell; Million+; 1994; University Alliance; UKADIA), with each of these further subdivided on the basis of dimensions of their strategic plans. The rationale for these decisions is based on differences in university goals, stakeholders, resources and environment, all of which will have a bearing on what it

	means to be a learning organization and how far that can be achieved.
Refine data collection and analysis methods	Content analysis of 15 university websites, followed by more detailed discourse analysis of parts of the websites of 5 of these.
Consider appropriate theoretical lens and rationale for it	Social practice theory takes the concept of the learning organization beyond idealised criteria.
Reconsider research design if necessary	Social practice theory addresses recurrent practices, values and attitudes. Therefore empirical data will be required generating detailed qualitative data.
Consider title for project	*"Reconceptualising the Concept of 'Learning Organization' for the UK Higher Education Context: Applying a social practice approach"*
Develop an account of the significance of the project in terms of original contribution to knowledge	Develops the notion of the 'learning organization' in a way which is applicable to and valuable for UK higher education. Applies the social practice lens to critique some earlier approaches to the concept of the 'learning organization' and show how it can be developed. Theoretical work has significance for the practices of universities working towards enhancing the organizational learning that occurs in those contexts.

Developing an Eye for a Workable Proposal

Assessing a research project proposal is a skill that develops with practice and improves with experience. Tacit knowledge is built up over time by reading proposals, by discussing them with others and by comparing one's own views to those of others. Much of supervision is tacit knowledge which can only be accumulated with experience. Backhouse (2009, p. 186) quotes a doctoral supervisor saying:

> …you develop a sense of where it's going wrong and where it's not, I can pick it up immediately, and that kind of expertise is not something that you can learn, you know, it's experience.

She also quotes a PhD candidate describing two academics talking on successive days, sketching a possible research project:

> …you walk down the passage, and you would see the same two people standing at the doorway talking about something and every day you'd walk past, they'd just talk for fifteen minutes in the morning, and every day when you walk past you'd catch a little of the conversation. Literally four days later, they'd posted that article on the archive and I was like, "Wow, now that's how it should be done." And it seemed like there was just such a wealth of ideas….but [also] the experience to say, "That one is worth pursuing. That one, I don't think is going to work. (Backhouse, 2009, p. 210).

High risk and low risk proposals
However, it is sometimes worth taking a risk.

Some proposals are not particularly solid in the sense that a 'successful' outcome seems less than highly probably. They might, though, offer the potential of coming up with something highly original, or approaching a problem in a way that non-one has done before. These are high(er) risk proposals and should not be discounted: tacit knowledge and wisdom are also applied in balancing risk with potential gain.

Below I offer some genuine examples of doctoral research proposals, with my commentary on them. I suggest reading them and, preferably, discussing them with others to develop a view. My view on each is only one perspective: readers may well disagree.

I'd like to offer heartfelt thanks the authors of the proposals for permission to reproduce them here. In some cases I have edited the proposal for concision and to enhance anonymity, including removing bibliographies and appendices.

Sample Proposal 1

Communities, Networks and Education

Abstract

This paper is an overview of my PhD research proposal. It is concerned with investigating evolving notions and expressions of community and networks in the context of educational culture which is engaged in the process of discovering the opportunities and challenges presented by Communications and Information Technologies (CITs). Parallel to this is the task of identifying key elements or threads that might be common to a wide diversity of educational "electronic communities". The research is further focused on a theme of "the changing paradigm", particularly within higher education, which runs through and across technological, organisational and academic domains. One perspective on this is articulated by the Vice Chancellor of the University of Melbourne Alan Gilbert when he argued in his keynote speech in November 1996 at The Virtual University? Symposium:

> ... the first step to survival is to ensure that the information superhighway runs through every great campus, and the second is to ensure that the riches it brings are in turn enriched in a real learning community.

The notion of "learning community" is one that will therefore form a locus for this research. In pursuing this, many so-called online learning communities will be analysed in terms of their creation and stated mission, development and methods for determining their effectiveness or otherwise. Following, in particular the theoretical model of Tiffin and Rajasingham, a range of case-studies will be presented.

However, at this early stage of the research...the primary case-study is concerned with the development of Education Network Australia (EdNA). EdNA is a government-sponsored "meta-network" launched in Australia in 1997 primarily as an online Information Directory Service — although its beginnings were some two years earlier, when it was conceived more in terms of connectivity and infrastructure. In its current (early) stage of development its foundations have firmed as a framework geared toward fostering collaboration and co-operation throughout the various Australian education and training sectors — that is, schools, vocational education and training, adult and community education, and higher education. In order to develop, it has had to adopt principles of exclusion (as well as inclusion) in order to provide only "quality" online educational resources for its constituency. In this process, *identity* is a key success factor.

Keywords
Community; Networks; Identity; EdNA

1. Introduction

The purpose of the study is to identify key elements or threads that might be common to a wide diversity of "electronic communities" operating within educational contexts. Such communities can express themselves as an outcome of extending the forum for interaction of an existing co-located community or workgroup, or more typically, as a self-sustaining "virtual" association existing across geographical, cultural, and timezone boundaries.

Why this focus?

Communications and Information Technologies (CITs) can be enabling tools which provide opportunities for communication and interaction which have not hitherto been possible.

It does not follow, however, that these tools are intrinsically enabling and, in fact, evidence suggests that contrary scenarios proliferate. [2,11] Notwithstanding this constraint, CITs have been, and are, fundamental to the emergence and development of so-called "electronic communities", "virtual communities", online "learning communities," and other associated collaborative and co-operative activities which occur in online environments (with "online" being used here in its broad and common usage to include both synchronous and asynchronous computer networks). The communications cultures evolving with usage of these technologies are unprecedented and in educational settings pose transformative challenges to the established pedagogical and organisational cultures [4]. Thus, analysis of these cultures will likely result in the "discovery" of a range of new practices being implemented in response and may further assist in the formulation of educational paradigms appropriate to them.

In the 1990s, concepts of "globalisation", "lifelong learning", and "just-in-time training" have become commonplace. These concepts are just a small set of an ever increasing lexicon associated with transition into the "information age" or "knowledge age" heralded by the "digital revolution".

At one extreme "the media" hypes up this process. It is itself fueled by its own vested interests in meeting this challenge, a challenge presented foremost by the "convergence" of digital technologies used in mass media distribution, telecommunications, computing, and, to some degree, education itself. At another extreme can be identified a paralysis or sluggishness in cultural response within higher education, both academically and organisationally, despite the surplus of "visionary" rhetoric.

Thus, this study must also closely monitor the evolution of concepts concerning "community" in the delivery of online education and services.

Of course, hand-in-hand with the evolution of language associated with these changes is the evolution of socio-cultural organisation. "Lifelong learning" and "just-in-time training" have become marketable slogans in an era where higher education is increasingly a mass market and a highly competitive proposition. Thus, notions of professional development as a process conducted in short bursts of intense professional learning that in turn punctuate longer cycles of "business as usual" in the workplace are also in question. This seems to be particularly so for educators: it is commonplace commentary that the balance in core activity of an educator is shifting from the "sage on the stage" to the "guide on the side".

2. Research/conceptual context

It is intended that appropriate theoretical/conceptual frameworks are researched and tested for their validity. Those that form the conceptual context for this investigation all intermesh to some degree. The primary sources forming the basis for this investigation include those of Berge and Collins [1], Castells [2], Tiffin and Rajasingham [14], Rheingold [12], Snyder [13], and Harasim et al. [6].

It is also anticipated that as the research proceeds the implied theoretical synthesis will need to be flexible so as to accommodate the rapid evolution of CITs and the educational communities and cultures which are adopting them.

While the Internet is clearly *the* Meta-Network of all meta-networks it is *identitification* with a particular community which can make an electronic network truly value-added and conducive toward collaboration.

In the case of EdNA, it is the education and training communities of Australia which serve to define the identity of the network — or more accurately, this meta-network since it brings together, and endeavours to promote collaboration across, several other large regional networks.

3. Research questions

From the literature survey (which includes ongoing access to online resources) a number of research questions have emerged — they are listed below in order of relevance, with the first two being fundamental:

1. How are concepts of "community" and "network" related in online environments?
2. What precisely constitutes a community in an online environment?
3. What factors constrain and what factors facilitate the evolution of community in online environments?
4. What conventional elements of community persist in online communities?
5. With the socio-cultural trend toward "lifelong learning" how is professional development for educators affected?
6. How does "virtual community" and the trend for "lifelong learning" interrelate?
7. Is a taxonomy of online "communities" possible?
8. How does hypermedia impact online *learning communities?*
9. How is organisational change within higher education impacting on educational practice?
10. Is the pursuit of collaboration and co-operation throughout and across the education and training sectors a flow-on effect from the enabling aspect of CITs? Or, is it more that these communities are somehow *compelled* to collaborate?

4. Research methods

In any PhD-related study *semantics* certainly demand that definitions are clarified. For example, depending from which vantage one looks from, a "community of networks" could also be viewed as a "network of communities". This blurring of semantics, however, also seems to be a feature of the object of study.

Following on from this and the questions outlined above there are also certain intrinsic difficulties concerning rigorous methodological study of the subject. This is certainly a common caveat for academic papers presented at IT-related conferences (e.g., see Roger Clarke's paper at CAUSE 97).

A diversity of university domains and "communities of practitioners" are investigated:

- subject-based electronic forums in higher education
- interest groups / newsgroups
- educational workgroups
- campus-based university electronic forums
- a "flexible-access" university (aka "open", "distance-education", "virtual")
- EdNA
- international higher educational consortia such as Universitas 21.

Note – the rest of the proposal, about the EdNA case study, and the reference list have been omitted for concision.

Commentary on sample proposal 1

There are some interesting and illuminative ideas here. The author comes across as keen and knowledgeable. However the proposal itself suffers from some major flaws:

1. The title doesn't contain a problematic or indicate a direction for the research. It doesn't indicate that the research focuses on communications and information technologies, even.

2. The abstract is too long (for an abstract) and contains a quote and details which do not belong there. Sequentially four areas of research are introduced but not linked to each other

adequately. The first one (beginning "It is concerned with…") is obscurely written. The second (beginning "Parallel to this…") is not specific – what kind of "elements or threads" are being investigated? The third ("The research is further focused…") makes an assumption that there is a changing paradigm but does not indicate its nature, only where it manifests. The fourth ("In pursuing this…") does not explain why the intention expressed is linked to the preceding material. In short, there is a sense of disconnection and a potentially limitless agenda.

3. The abstract also gives the impression that the research is uncritically accepting the agenda of the Vice-Chancellor quoted and of EdNA, rather than being an independent research project which develops its own set of issues.

4. After setting out a very large scope for the research in the abstract, the Introduction shrinks the research agenda to the second of the four objectives set out in the abstract. However, under the heading Why This Focus? a fifth purpose is introduced: to discover new practices being implemented and so assisting in the formulation of educational paradigms appropriate to them. Later, a sixth purpose is revealed: "closely monitor[ing] the evolution of concepts concerning 'community'…" By now the scope of the project is completely out of hand.

5. Under the heading Research/conceptual context it is not explained why the work of the authors mentioned might be relevant to this research. It is not clear whether or not they are commensurable and so able to be integrated into an illuminative whole, theoretically.

6. The research questions finally appear after several pages. There are far too many, some are far too ambitious (especially the penultimate one) and they have only a partial connection to what has been said previously in the proposal.

7. The Research methods section contains very little detail of the design: no specifics are provided.

So, there are plenty of good ideas here. But revising this proposal to provide one which is focused and deliverable needs to start with revising the research questions. They should be reduced in number and scope. Then a research design should be provided which is detailed and specific. That design should clearly have the potential to deliver answers to the research questions. There is no need for an abstract in a research proposal; the proposal itself should be a very condensed outline of the project. And it needs to provide the reader with a very solid grasp of what will happen, and why.

So what might a revised set of research questions look like? Any revisions need to result in questions which:
- Are of interest
- Answerable
- Move from the descriptive to the analytical and explanatory
- Provide an original contribution to knowledge when answered.

I would suggest the following as a first attempt:

"This multi-site case study research project examines the nature of interactions and discourse used in online learning groups to answer the following research questions set out below.

In 12 online learning groups in different disciplines and institutional contexts:

1. How does the concept of "community" manifest itself and develop?
2. What factors inhibit and promote the development of an online "community" in its various senses?

3. What are the effects of the development of online community (in the senses developed in answering research question 1) in terms of learning, interactions and discourse?
4. What are the implications of the answers to the above for policy and practice in higher education institutions at different levels, including institutional policy and learning design?

Sample Proposal 2

Title

Mobile-based Communities of Practice for History in Higher Education in the Universities of Anon1(Private) and the University of Anon2(Public), an East African country.

Aims/Objectives:

This research will investigate, prototype, and disseminate the findings of a mobile-based community of practice for History in higher education in the universities of Anon1(Private) and the University of Anon2(Public). The purpose of this research is to not only analyze and document requirements on the impact of mobile-based environments for disciplinary practice, but to determine if these environments can support the reflective, multimodal, and collaborative knowledge construction demanded by the practice of History in higher education.

Research Questions

Are mobile-based communities of practice able to meet the disciplinary processes for collaboration, reflection, knowledge production and dissemination for the practice of History in higher education in an East African country?

What effect does a mobile-based community of practice for History in higher education in an East African country have on the production and dissemination of disciplinary knowledge (journals, monographs, posts, interaction, etc.)?

Can any developed mobile-based community of practice that meets these disciplinary needs be community organized and designed in an East African country?

Background to the Research

It is the intended goal of this research to critically explore the potential of constructing a community of practice (History) in higher education in an East African country based primarily in a mobile environment. This goal is based on the assumption that the most commonly available mobile technology in the target area in question are SMS-enabled phones. Therefore, this research will investigate SMS-based services for creating mobile communities of practice.

In keeping with what Goodyear (2004) refers to as networked learning, a mobile-based community of practice is used to promote connections between learners and foster communities which make efficient use of their resources. The establishment of a community of History in a mobile environment is intended to serve the disciplinary practices of History in higher education by being collaborative in knowledge discussion, reflective in knowledge construction, and authoritative in knowledge dissemination.

As such, this mobile community of practice will target practitioners of History (either faculty, or graduate level students) in higher education in the University of Anon2(Public) and the universities of Anon1(Private).

History is chosen primarily due to the absence of expert-level mobile learning frameworks and applications for university level education in both developed and developing nations.

In short, very little research has been conducted to determine whether mobile learning in History is a suitable vehicle for higher education in developing nations; a framework will be applied to assess whether this is indeed possible, whether a mobile-based community of interest in History can support reflective and collaborative knowledge construction consistent with the disciplinary practices of History. There are several reasons for this choice of location (an East African country), including the following:

- History as contested knowledge (relationship between Anon1(Private) and an East African country; post-colonialism and national identity: What does it mean to be an East African country?
- Gap (economically, politically, and culturally) between Anon1(Private) and mainland East African country and the potential for mobile networks to bridge these divides
- An East African country's presence within the East African Community (EAC).

It is my belief that mobile environments for disciplinary practice in higher education in Anon1(Private) and throughout East African country can serve to explore and potentially mitigate the gap between Anon1(Private) and mainland an East African country through renewed dialogue and networking practitioners of History; through this renewed dialogue, history as a contested subject will be explored leading, potentially, to a renewed focus on post-colonialism and national identity.

National identity, in particular, represents a developmental need as both Anon1(Private) and an East African country explore the efficiency and long-term future of their political union. This research explicitly attempts to network the community of practice for History in higher education in Anon1(Private) with that of the leading university on the East African country's mainland, the University of Anon2(Public).

Theories

Much instructional pedagogy in History in higher education is constructivist in nature. Constructivist frameworks of instruction stress the role of context and social negotiation of knowledge in instruction (Savery, Duffy, 1996).

History establishes context through its pursuit of knowledge claims, their validation, and the manner of practices associated with this process. The social negotiation of knowledge is established through the apprenticeship model in higher education, namely the pairing of a student (apprenticing historian) with a mentor (practicing historian). Mobile learning's affordance for this context and social negotiation will be analyzed to determine its applicability to the practice of History in higher education.

Building on this constructivist pedagogy, the work of Meyer and Land in regards to threshold concepts offers considerable insight into the practice of History in higher education (2005). Meyer and Land's analysis of the role of 'thresholds' in developing "pedagogically fertile" and role-defining shifts in learner's understanding of their place as active members of the discipline has great application for History as the vehicle for disciplinary understanding (Meyer, Land, 374).

All of the participants in this research are active members of the History discipline, at varying stages of development (student vs. faculty, university vs. research organization) and at varying degrees of affiliation with their institution and their profession.

This self-perception of thinking "like a historian" has value pedagogically as an instrument that motivates participation and collaboration (Enwistle, 2005, 8).

The experience of 'legitimate peripheral participation' in the work of the professional historian is constructivist in nature, emphasizing as it does collaborative knowledge construction.

It further is identity forming by establishing etiquette for "communicating ideas in academically acceptable forms of expression and argument" (2005, 8).

Students are taught to act, argue, participate, and express themselves as historians. The pedagogical importance placed on disciplinary participatory identity in History emphasizes the importance of establishing the level of receptiveness to mobile learning on a disciplinary level. With so much emphasis placed on identity as a historian, viewing their receptiveness to mobile learning as partly influenced by disciplinary norms is prudent.

"Towards a Theory of Mobile Learning" provides a useful mediation between learning and technology and will be used to analyze mobile learning for History (Sharples, 2005).

Sharples builds on the work of Pask (Conversation Theory) and Engestrom (expansive activity model) by establishing mobile learning as an engagement with technology, "in which tools such as computers and mobile phones function as interactive agents in the process of coming to know, creating a human-technology system to communicate, to mediate agreements between learners and to aid recall and reflection" (Sharples, 2005, 7).

Further, the work of Sharples, Taylor, and Vavoula offers an evaluation of any potential mobile learning solution, an additional framework that can be applied to this research (2007). This work posits mobile learning in terms of its affordance for mobility, its identification of learning as a constructive and social process, and the role of situated activity mediated by technology (Sharples, Taylor, Vavoula, 2007, 225).

Any potential mobile environment derived from this research will be gauged based on its ability to satisfy these facets of mobile learning.

Sharples' work will be used as an instrument to determine whether mobile learning for History creates control (both the community of learners and their association with higher education), context (in terms of the learning activities and objects) and communication (in mobile learning's ability to allow for communication both within the learning community and the ability to disseminate communication to the greater academic community)

Sample

The participant group will be drawn from faculty and graduate students in the departments of History at the following universities. The potential size of a participant group will range from 30 to 60 participants, depending on willingness to participate.

- Anon1(Private) University
- University of Anon2(Public)
- Anon3(Private) University

Methods

The research methods used for this exploration of mobile communities of practice for History in higher education in an East African country will involve both quantitative and qualitative elements. The research will begin with communication with select faculty and students at the two selected universities in Anon1(Private) to determine the validity of disciplinary assumptions put forth in this research proposal. This communication will be used to reconfigure disciplinary practice for History in an East African country if necessary.

Based on this initial feedback, a participatory design process will be employed with participants to determine the needs, requirements, and cultural, emotional, or social variables that might affect participation in any mobile community of practice. This participatory design process will inform a conceptual design of a mobile environment for the practice of History in higher education. Subsequent assessment of this design will be tied to fulfilling the needs of disciplinary practice in History (epistemology, ontology, knowledge construction, collaboration, reflection, and dissemination) as well as the ability of the design to assist "in the process of coming to know, creating a human-technology system to communicate, to mediate agreements between learners and to aid recall and reflection" (Sharples, 2005).

Methodology
This research will employ a mixed-methods approach. Quantitative elements will involve analysis of participant demographic and technological use information, as well as communication patterns within and without their respective Departments of History. Qualitative facets will involve interviews and their subsequent narrative analysis, as well as the participatory design process sessions, which will be recorded and subjected to a narrative analysis as well.

This combination of qualitative and quantitative aspects is intended to determine disciplinary process, represent that disciplinary process in a designed mobile environment, and to gauge potential impact of such an environment on disciplinary knowledge production.

Data Analysis
Quantitative data collected from communication, surveys, and participatory design phases will be analyzed to determine quantity of communication within respective departments of

History at the three focus universities, and across these departments. Quantitative data will be analyzed to determine number of collaborative interactions amongst participants towards knowledge production. Further, a prototype will be evaluated to determine its satisfaction of design requirements and disciplinary process. Qualitative data will be collected from preliminary communication, interview transcripts, and recorded transcripts from participatory design sessions; these will be subjected to a narrative analysis. Narrative analysis is an attempt to follow the participants "down their trails", to give participants an authentic voice in dictating their own receptiveness to mobile communities of practice (Riessman 2008). This authenticity helps elicit the autobiographical-self (2008). This narrative empowerment will hopefully reveal elements of autonomy and investment in the mobile environment that would have otherwise gone unnoticed.

Task Description Timeframe

1. Preliminary communication: identify/communicate with faculty and students in History Identify sample group, collect participant information, areas of research expertise, levels of communication with historical community, commitment to this project -2 months

2. Survey - Survey designed to collect information on technology use, gauge the validity of assumptions on the disciplinary practices- 1month

3. Interviews-assess the validity of the disciplinary practices of History, modes of collaboration and knowledge production- 3 months

4. Narrative Analysis of Interview Transcripts- conduct narrative analysis on interview transcripts to gauge narrative of professional interaction and satisfaction-3 months

5. Participatory Design and Conceptual Prototyping Multiple (on-site) sessions to develop needs assessments, requirements, and prototype mobile environment-3-6 months
6. Assessment of Mobile Environments for the practice of History in higher education in an East African country-Dissertation writing phase-12 months

Commentary on sample proposal 2

As is frequently the case with proposal titles, this one contains no problematic – no clue as to the central issue being addressed. Apart from being uninformative to the reader, this absence suggests a lack of focus on the part of the writer, which is not a good start.

The proposal does however have strength in situating the research questions early and giving a clear feel for the nature of the project. However it reads as though the project will be a form of action research, confirmed by the early use of the word 'prototype' as a verb. However that phrase (action research) is not used. There are hints that the research will be centrally involved in the development project described, but this is never brought out.

Nor is there any suggestion of which 'flavour' of action research this might be, whether there will be interventions at different points by the researcher, with effects evaluated and so on.

This is potentially a very interesting and useful [action] research project, but the relationship between the development project and the research project is only tangentially described, and the wider significance of the research project to the research community is not addressed at all.

A reader might be forgiven for concluding that this research will mostly be of benefit to the online community described; and this is inadequate for a PhD. However there is in fact greater potential in the project.

There is, from time to time, something of a missionary feel to the proposal – for example in the sentence beginning "it is my belief...." This is another danger sign because it suggests that the researcher's mind is already made up before the research has been done. It also adds confirmation to the potential impression that as a research and development project, this is more development than research.

There is some confusion about how many universities are involved in the design for this research. Most often it is two. But in two places in the proposal three universities are mentioned. This kind of instability is, of course, not good. Unless there is some specific and limited purpose for the inclusion of the third. If so, this is not explained.

To conclude, this is an interesting and potentially valuable project but the written proposal does not really do it justice.

Sample Proposal 3

Negotiating the Faultlines: A study of PhD development

The journey of development that researchers and scholars take within the institutional framework of the degree of Doctor of Philosophy has in the last ten years attracted the attention of both academic researchers and bureaucrats in Australia.

While some researchers (Neumann, 2003; McWilliam, Taylor et al, 2002) have been concerned with the institutional framework that supports the degree, others (Lee, 1998; Lee and Williams, 1999; Johnson et al, 2000; Macauley, 2001; Vilkinas, 2005) have been more interested in what the experience of individual students reveals about both supervision pedagogy and the dominant discourses within academia concerning this highest rank of examinable degrees.

No study has thus far followed and tracked a group of candidates through their degrees, perhaps because until now there has not been an easy way for a group of candidates to interact and share their experiences as they happen. The development of software that supports the real-time online recording of events as they happen, a process called web logging (colloquially known as blogging), has now made a longitudinal study of this kind possible. This study proposes to create a community of PhD candidates who are prepared to both maintain blogs themselves and to read and comment on the blogs maintained by the other members of the study group.

My own experience in teaching and researching both academic writing and online learning, my reading about graduate pedagogy, my thinking about the nature of the PhD process, about the growing phenomenon of blogging, and about how university communities reproduce themselves and generate knowledge has lead me to my research question:

To what extent can PhD candidates be sustained in their development as researchers through the use of blogging?

The research question will be answered by analysis of the blogs – the body of narrative that the candidates produce, in which they will reveal to themselves and to the group both *what* and *how* they are learning in their own reflections and ongoing narratives. Although the content matter of the thesis-writing process that each is engaged in will be individual and unique, they will share the experience of *doing* the PhD to *become* a doctor– their working toward a common goal in perhaps the most complex project that most of them have ever attempted.

Blogs have been described by Williams and Jacobs (2004, p232) as having 'the capacity to engage people in collaborative activity, knowledge sharing, reflection and debate, where complex and expensive technology has failed'. A blog is not only a space to write, but also a place to store and display pictures and graphics and make lists of links to useful references, to your work in progress, and to work completed.

A blog is thus more like a cyber-desk than just a place to make and store notes, and a blog's ability to be shared adds the dimension of an ongoing conversation – the cyberdesk has a place for passers-by to add their comments to what they read, and in this study it is intended that the blogs of group members will be open to each other for comments, and that the blogs will be the tool for community building within the group.

Although academic thinking about the uses of blogs in higher education is in its infancy, these uses are also continually being charted, discussed, predicted, reported and glossed in detail on blogs such as Weblogs in Higher Education. ...This tendency of blogs to comment on and aggregate the contents of other blogs is often referred to as 'the blogosphere'.

The non-educational social nature of blogging has been explored by Nardi et al (2004) who claim that "blogs create the audience, but the audience also creates the blog". Their study of 23 social blogs maintained by university students, graduates and graduate students also found that the social dimension of blogging made blogs much more than online diaries; they classified the motivations that bloggers had to continue their blogging activities as to (p4):

1. update others on activities and whereabouts
2. express opinions to influence others
3. seek others' opinions and feedback
4. "think by writing"
5. release emotional tension

With the possible exception of the first item in this list, which is the most transparent motivation for anyone to keep a blog, each of these objectives will provide a dimension in this study on the socialization of PhD candidates into academic argumentation and research culture. Certainly the last two are particularly interesting in the terms of Lee's writing about both the place of writing in the creation of 'the doctor' (1998, 2003) and the 'distress' inherent in the PhD process in Australia (Lee and Williams, 1999).

Johnson et al (2000) explore the development of the 'autonomous researcher' in the terms of the traditional model of PhD pedagogy, which Leder (1995) refers to as having an 'apprentice-like' quality. Its fundamental aim was to teach candidates independence, using techniques that mostly amounted to varying degrees of abandonment.

However, scholars who have challenged these practices and attempted to undertake a more pastoral supervisory role report being overwhelmed by the needs of their students. Johnson et al suggest that autonomy may need to be *developed* in candidates, rather than *revealed*, and point out that "new modes of knowledge production"(p143) and the current trend toward more collaborative production of knowledge within universities will require that researchers have more skills in collaboration, supported as they are, increasingly, by joint process.

This proposed more constructivist approach to postgraduate pedagogy has echoes in the theories of how people learn online.
Most successful online learning is associated with constructivist pedagogies (Maor & Zabriski 2003).
The well-known and often-repeated advice to teachers going online that they will have to move from their position as the 'sage on the stage' to the 'guide on the side' implies the pedagogical position that students learning online are constructing their own knowledge from the available information, rather than accepting their knowledge whole from 'the master'.

The development of blogs and wikis (online encyclopaedias with open authorship) as educational tools has the potential to reduce the role of the 'guide on the side' even further – perhaps online teachers, like the absent supervisors reported in so many studies of doctoral candidate development, are now becoming 'the ghost with no post'.

While those words are mine, the fear that teachers will largely disappear from education is often related to the development of educational technology without an attendant pedagogical framework (eg, Taylor 1995). Students working online can be left to share, discuss, problem-solve, and develop their own knowledge from sources of information that are now vast – indeed they sometimes seem almost limitless. They must learn to judge the validity of what they find for themselves, and to develop the skills necessary to defend their positions within and through a group of people whom they may never see face-to-face. The (often misunderstood) role of 'guide on the side' is crucial to the success of this kind of educational setting (Salmon 1999, 2002).

Economic pressure rather than pedagogical preference is often the driver for institutional movement toward online teaching. It is also economic pressure that has raised the interest of both bureaucrats and academics in postgraduate pedagogy: pressure to lift completion rates has conflicted with increased time pressure on academics and an expressed wish by some academics for a 'softer', more supportive model for PhD supervision (Johnson et al, 2000).

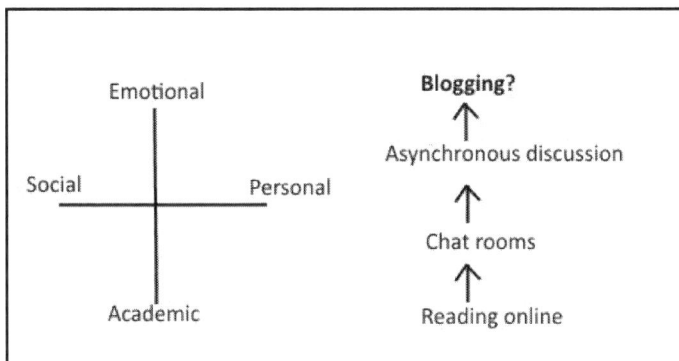

Figure 1: The pedagogy of cyber learning

Figure 1 uses a theory of online pedagogy to show how blogging might support the development of candidates. As online tasks move from academic engagement in reading material that has been placed online, through the social engagement of chat rooms and the more thoughtful and reflective work that results from reading and contributing to asynchronous discussion, participants move toward involving their emotions in the learning experience (Salmon, 1999).

It is this involvement of the emotional dimension that has been identified by Green and Lee (1998) and by Johnson et al (2000) as the most under theorised part of PhD pedagogy. The use of blogging over time in this study will provide an online environment that will enable trust to build in the community, so that participants can establish emotional connections and relate in new and unpredictable ways.

A community of blogging PhD candidates would bring together people who are learning how to become – how to negotiate for themselves the building of the identity of 'doctor' both against and within disciplinary cultures and institutional strictures that can be traced back to the ideas of Voltaire and Rousseau (Johnson et al, 2000). Supervisors, of course, are themselves the product of this process and have been profoundly influenced by their own process of self-creation in their doctoral role. This study will contribute to the complex question of how pedagogy can be understood within the supervisor/candidate relationship as discussed by Green and Lee (1995), and, most importantly, will be understood and enacted in the university of the future. At the heart of these issues lie the questions posed at the end of their article (p44):

- How is pedagogy to be best understood, in all its complexity and necessity, within the symbolic-disciplinary economy of the Academy?
- What stories (and counter-stories) need to be told?

- What spaces are there for different practices and voices in post-graduate contexts, including research in and for postgraduate studies and pedagogy?
- What new imaginings are necessary for teaching and research in and for the emerging postmodern university?

Despite the differences in epistemologies that have often been categorised across disciplines (eg, Becher and Trowler, 2001), the blogging by individuals of the common ground of their struggle (which may, in any discipline, involve 'distress', according to Lee and Williams, 1999) will create shared narratives of development. Wenger (1998) describes how people working on a shared trajectory toward a common goal contribute and create meaning and identity by sharing the unfolding narratives of their experience.

The application of Wenger's theory to candidates for the PhD degree may not seem immediately obvious. The work he did to develop his theory was done in an insurance company, with workers doing a set of apparently routinised tasks – but whose day-to-day work often involved dealing with phone calls from angry and resentful members of the public, raising the kinds of uncertainty and anxiety that no amount of routine can protect you from.

In his 1998 book Wenger describes how, as a group, the workers formed an unofficial 'community of practice' to share and create knowledge that would help them as individuals make sense of the sometimes Kafkaesque situations they found themselves in, due in most part to their inability to understand the complexities of unexplained arcane practices within the insurance industry, or even, to some degree, the dense administrative structures of their own employer.

[Wenger] develops this theory into areas of negotiation of meaning and development of identity in groups where people work together to make sense of what is happening to them. He then develops this theory into areas of institutional development and educational design.

The endeavour of attaining a doctorate, which is both cognitive and experiential, in fact lends itself well to the application of Wenger's construction of a community of practice. PhD candidates are working in an area in which development although often understood as prescriptive, is also, somehow, mysterious.

If Wenger's conception of 'community' is understood in the context of a dynamic (but, note, not necessarily always peaceful or agreeable) quest for meaning being created by its members through the exchange of ideas, insights and understandings, then his notion can be applied to a group of people who are sharing the process of attaining a doctorate.

Wenger's words 'shared trajectory', are also not entirely transparent. They imply flight in the same direction toward a fixed target. But Wenger's use of the word 'trajectory' is more complex than this: "The term trajectory suggests not a path that can be foreseen or charted but a continuous motion – one that has a momentum of its own in addition to a field of influences (p154)." The group that will form the core of this study is not a planned or formulaic entity. Its members will not answer questionnaires, nor will they participate in surveys or take part in focus groups. They will write themselves into the study and it will be what it becomes.

Aims

The central aim of the research is to follow and report on the process of what Lee (1998) calls the making of 'a newly licensed kind of person, a "doctor"', and to investigate the effects of the use of blogging by candidates on this process.

Objectives
The research has three objectives:

- To investigate cybergroup formation and its effect on participants' candidature
- To document the emotional life of and the process of self-discovery in a group of PhD candidates over time
- To encourage candidates in the study to use blogging to 'write themselves' into their own development and to create a community of practice through the use of shared blogs

Justification
This research is intended to track and report on the experiences of a diverse group of PhD candidates in real time over two years. While some work has been done in Australia directly on the experiences of completing a PhD (Lee and Williams 1999; Neumann 2003), most has relied on the recall and reported memory of successful candidates, or one-off interviews with current candidates. Macauley (1990) had his subjects, both candidates and supervisors, complete two questionnaires and a series of in-depth interviews. More recently, Vilkinas (2005) has collected the stories of present candidates at a point in their thesis task.

None of the previous studies into the process of PhD formation in Australia have used a longitudinal method nor have they maintained contact with students over even a short time.

Neumann uses 'slice of time' techniques, interviewing around 100 students at differing stages of their projects from a range of different disciplines.

She uses Becher and Trowler's quadrant model (2001) to classify disciplines into hard, soft, pure, and applied, and also classified students according to their full-time or part-time enrolment and as early, mid or late stage candidates. The results can be taken as accurate at a point in time, but not offering any new insight into the overall PhD process for candidates.

Lee and Williams (1999) used techniques of memory work, asking six academics to draw on their memories of their own PhDs, and narrative writing to report on these memories.
The subjects in this pilot are current academics – meaning previous candidates who have completed a PhD successfully, and who were undoubtedly informed in their narratives by their later roles as supervisors. The rather dramatic revelations in this article concerning the distress that the memory work revealed raised the questions listed on page 4 above. Vilkinas, using similar self-reporting but by current candidates, also raises questions of emotionality in her recent book. However, her contributors, again, were writing at a point in time rather than over a protracted period.

Macauley (2001) used questionnaires and in depth interviews with existing students. Although he has made a valuable contribution to viewing the transition to independent scholarship in Australian universities, he is still seeing the process in fairly standard 'growing up' terms, relying heavily on a distinction between pedagogy and andragogy to measure the maturation of candidates as scholars.

So, while all of these studies have reported to a more or less extent on the emotionality of the PhD experience, none has created and reported on a narrative of experience distilled from real-time reflection, nor have any of them attempted to create a community of candidates.

Methodology

This study will be a qualitative one. The research question will be answered by thematic analysis of the body of narrative that the candidates produce – we will reveal to ourselves and to the group both *what* and *how* we are learning in our own reflections and ongoing narratives.

Although the content matter of the thesis-writing process that each of us is engaged in will be individual and unique, we will share the experience of 'doing' the PhD – our working toward a common goal in perhaps the most complex project that most of us have ever attempted. The endeavour of attaining a doctorate, which is both cognitive and experiential, lends itself well to the application of Wenger's construction of a community of practice, within which he suggests people both bring and create meaning and identity for themselves.

The study will be a reflective ethnography, my own development as a scholar being a part of the process of doing the study. I will be a fully participating member of the online group, and open about my role as a researcher, so I will be a participant-observer (Erlandson et al, 1993, p96). Sometimes it may be difficult or impossible for me to separate my roles as subject and object in my own study – but except in the case of disrespectful or disruptive behaviour as discussed below, I will resist as far as possible the role of 'group leader'. I will also resist as far as possible the urge to 'spark up' blog postings during quiet periods – although this may prove very difficult if the flow of material is so low as to threaten the project!

As an ethnographer, the place in which my study will be conducted will be cyberspace. Visualisations of the World Wide Web and the 'reality' of cyberspace and the human interactions that take place in it has been canvassed by researchers in such sites as Cyber Geography Research.

Candidates will be recruited through post-graduate student organizations.

To some extent they may be self-selecting, as they will almost certainly be technologically confident (although there is no reason why even inexperienced people cannot learn to blog), and commitment to the group may at times seem high. However, I hope that membership of the group will also be seen as conveying benefits for participants in peer support and development through their personal writing.

The number of participants in this study will be small – no more than 20 people. They will be broadly-discipline based, and should cover as wide a range of methodologies and branches of academic research as possible. They will need to be prepared to share honestly and freely, and have some commitment to the group's trajectory as well as to their own progress.

Ethics and anticipated difficulties
The identities of candidates in the group will be hidden from each other. Nicknames will be used, and in the reporting process the candidates will be classified according to their methodologies and Becher and Trowler's (2001) quadrant of discipline groupings (cf Neumann 2003), not by their actual discipline.

I am more interested in knowing whether a student is doing bench-top research or undertaking surveys and focus groups than I am in whether she is a scientist, a social scientist or a philosopher.

Candidates will also be asked to not give their supervisors' names if they need to post about exchanges with them, but rather to use a predesignated nickname.

It will be impressed upon group members that all blog entries and comments are not to be copied or commented on elsewhere.

Any instances of material posted within the group appearing elsewhere will result in the offender being removed from the study and thus from access to the blogs.

A constant possibility in online groups is the activity of personal flaming (abusive language) and other destructive online activities causing disruption and even temporary or permanent breakdown of a group. In blogs, abusive or hurtful or hateful comments can be left. I have been a member of dozens of online discussion groups of a different kinds since 1996; I have taught academic writing for two years using online discussion groups as the main mode of content delivery, and have moderated hobby-based email discussion groups. I have always successfully practised a low-tolerance policy for behaviour that denotes disrespect for group members. While some allowance can be made for highly charged emotional states from time to time, this behaviour cannot be allowed to damage the trust that holds the group together. In this case participants will each own their own blog, and will always be completely free to remove any comments from their blogs if they wish. Anonymous commenting will not be allowed, so repeat offenders can be removed from the group. This policy will be detailed on the candidate information sheet.

There could be some difficulties arising from resistance or defensiveness on the part of supervisors, who could view the project as somehow undermining their position or even reputation by the 'gossipy' nature of a closed group. This could be countered by a clear explanation of the importance of confidentiality and the way that candidate identities will be hidden, and the preparation of a detailed supervisor information sheet to accompany the candidate information sheet.

Finally, there may be unexpected problems in my own life as I undertake this PhD. If at times I am not able to participate in the group, this will not pose a problem. I can continue to monitor blog postings in case of problems, but the group should be able to function for some time without my constant input.

Provisional work schedule
Second half of 2005: preparing and gaining ethics approval – part-time
2006-2007:   the blogs are being created – part-time
2008-2009:   thematic analysis and thesis writing –full-time

Resource requirements
Technical support for blogging – to be investigated. Although the university IT service does not currently offer blogging software here are several sites that offer free blogging services that can be password protected from the wider world.

Outlay would be minimal.

Commentary on sample proposal 3

This looks like a very interesting doctorate in prospect. The proposal begins with a convincing overview of some literature and quickly establishes a gap in the research which this project will fill ("No study has thus far followed and tracked...."). The first, impressive, paragraph would have been stronger had it finished by not only saying that a community of PhD candidates will be created, but to say why.

The first couple of paragraphs give the distinct impression that this is more a development project than a research one, and so a question mark begins to form around the issue of whether this is actually *doctoral* research being described. The research question which follows those paragraphs also appears to be developmental rather than a doctoral research question. Fortunately the rest of the proposal dispels this impression to a large extent, but it's best not to let it form in the first place. Readers will now be asking: "so what is the greater relevance to the academic community being offered here?"

A further common problem with doctoral proposals concerning technology is what might be called "tech-centrism". By this is meant too much focus on, and excitement about, a particular piece of, or use of technology, with an attendant loss of focus on the research issues. Another consequence can be lack of realism about the potential benefits of the technology, associated with an unwillingness to see negative aspects.

There is some evidence of this in the paragraph beginning "Blogs have been described…" and in later parts of the proposal. An example later in the proposal is the sentence which runs "The use of blogging over time in this study will provide an online environment that will enable trust to build in the community, so that participants can establish emotional connections and relate in new and unpredictable ways."

After the list of 5 motivations that bloggers may have there is quite a long section which, while well-informed and interesting, isn't adequately related to the group of bloggers to be created for the research, nor to the research project itself. There needs to be better linkage.

There is an important statement about the contributions that this research will make in the paragraph which begins "a community of blogging Ph.D. candidates". The sentence begins: "this study will contribute to the complex question ....". This section should be highlighted because it puts to rest, partly at least, the "so-what?" question about the significance of this research.

The structure of the proposal becomes a little strange towards the end. Beginning with the heading "Aims" there is considerable repetition and some material that really belonged much earlier in the proposal, including the aims and objectives of the research. Locating the three bullet points of objectives set out near the end next to the research question which is articulated at the beginning would probably highlight the fact that there is something of a disconnect between them. The research question addresses the sustainability of candidates' development as researchers through the use of blogging whereas the objectives begin with that and extend it.

The development of further research questions is clearly necessary to address this and also to make concrete the very reasonable claims for wider significance that the proposal can make.

The final problem arises in the last four paragraphs. Here, suddenly, the researcher is positioned as part of the group doing the blogging for the first time, though it is unclear whether the researcher will also be a doctoral candidate or will be their teacher in some sense (the phrase "group leader" is used).

An additional data collection method is introduced very near the end of the proposal, which appears to be some form of auto-ethnography.

There is a statement that the candidates will be recruited through post-graduate student organisations, which raises the question as to whether this group will be recruited from one university, or many. The details of sampling are thus occluded.

So this is potentially a valuable research project and a very interesting one. The proposal overall this convincing: clearly this person has some very concrete and well-developed ideas. The proposal, however, could be a lot better than it is.

Interestingly, the abstract of the successfully-completed doctorate based on this proposal is available on the web. While there are a few differences, both methodologically and in the in the use of theory, the finished doctorate is remarkably similar to the original proposal. This is not always the case.

Sample Proposal 4

(Written as part of an application to study)

Institutional Change in South Africa: Academic adaptation for improving the quality of Teaching and Learning. A case study of a South African university

The study would aim to explore the extent to which increasing external and internal pressures for institutional change have influenced the ways in which a well-resourced South African university has adapted its structures, policies and processes to achieve its strategic goals of improving the quality of teaching and learning.

The rationale for the study lies in the need for the post-1994 South African higher education system to be transformed from one that was shaped by discrimination and inequalities of class, race and gender under colonialism and apartheid to one that is inclusive and serves the needs of our diverse population and changing society.

In his framework for theorising about institutional change, Badat (2009: 457) has identified four dimensions of change: *the context, trajectory, dynamics and the determinants of change*. This study will necessarily consider the *context* of institutional change in South Africa and at the university itself as the apartheid social order and its priorities strongly impacted on the production of knowledge, teaching and learning and the curriculum and texts (ibid).

Since 1994, globalisation and its accompanying neoliberal ideology have impacted on institutional change by prioritising economic growth over redistributive policies and action. This has restricted the pace of change required and South Africa remains one of the most unequal societies in the world.

Commentary on sample proposal 4

1. The proposal looks good in terms of the thinking behind it and the thrust of the research. However the proposal is not punchy and specific enough.

2. The opening sentence is very long and wordy and hard to get a conceptual grip of, but it's an important one.

3. Words like 'explore' should be avoided - they are too open. The author should aim to give a very clear picture of the research to the reader, especially what the central problematic is.

4. There needs to be some specific research questions - and they need to be stated early.

5. The amount of time spent describing the literature should be reduced.

6. The author needs to be clear that s/he will use secondary data to situate the single-site case study within the context nationally

7. The actual study needs to be foregrounded in the proposal. Here it gets a paragraph towards the end. The aim is to give the reader a clear, early, idea of what the project is about.

8. The methods are also too vague. No clear idea is given of exactly what the research will look like.

9. State the purpose and the likely contribution explicitly - and embed them in research questions as far as possible. For example it seems likely that there be policy and practice implications for the case study university and or other universities as well as a contribution to the literature. There could be a research question about this.

Sample Proposal 4 (Revised)

(Revised and Extended Version after Feedback)

Institutional Change in South Africa: Academic adaptation for improving the quality of Teaching and Learning. A case study of a South African university

There is a widespread view in the higher education sector and broader society that transformation of the higher education sector and change within universities has been too slow and not kept pace with external and internal demands for change. Through an in-depth study of a well resourced university, this study examines this view systematically. In particular, the study will examine the extent to which increasing external and internal pressures for institutional change have influenced the ways in which this university has adapted its structures, policies and processes to achieve its strategic goals of improving the quality of teaching and learning.

The rationale for the study lies in the need for the post-1994 South African higher education system to be transformed from one that was shaped by discrimination and inequalities of class, race and gender under colonialism and apartheid to one that is inclusive and serves the needs of our diverse population and changing society.

Possible research questions:
- How have national policy interventions to improve the quality of teaching and learning within universities contributed to institutional change at the case study institution
- To what extent have the case study university's structures, policies and processes been adapted to achieve the goals of its Teaching and Learning Strategy?
- What opportunities have opened up for the case study university to improve student access and success through teaching and learning interventions?
- What are the constraints to improving the quality of teaching and learning within the institution?

The study will draw on the framework developed by Badat (2009: 457) who has identified four dimensions of change: *the context, trajectory, dynamics and the determinants of change*. The *context* of the apartheid social order and its priorities strongly impacted on the production of knowledge, teaching and learning and the curriculum and texts of South African universities (ibid). Since 1994, globalisation and its accompanying neoliberal ideology have prioritised economic growth over redistributive policies and action. This has restricted the pace of change required and South Africa remains one of the most unequal societies in the world.

The second dimension identified by Badat is the trajectory of change. Although political and socio-economic conditions may partly explain the reasons for change or a lack thereof in higher education, Badat argues that human agency is critical to understanding institutional change.

He asserts that "social agents and actors acting in cooperation and/or conflict within the system and the institutions" determine the pace, nature and outcomes. They influence the *trajectory of change* within institutions as they manage tensions between competing, values, goals and strategies in delivering on social equity and redress and economic development and quality. Badat has argued that often these social actors become the key policy-making actors and *determinants of change*. (2009: 456). It is important to note that institutional contexts differ vastly in the South African higher education system owing to the extremely differentiated system inherited from apartheid.

At the institutional level, the study will draw on the work of David Dill (1999) to understand the dynamics of change in the recently formalised areas of teaching and learning in South African higher education institutions. He has argued that in the competitive environment, universities have adapted their internal structures to enhance quality, promote interdisciplinary research and increase their entrepreneurial activities (1999). He reported that while patterns do exist between institutions, it is important to consider different institutional contexts. His work would be useful in the specific focus of this study, which is to examine the Teaching Development Grants (TDGs) as an instrument to promote the quality of teaching and learning at the case study university. The TDGs are funded by national government and more than 40 projects have been implemented across the university. New and adapted institutional structures and policies have emerged in order to meet the educational goals of the projects and the accountability requirements of the state.

This study will contribute to the improvement of specific policy and practice at the case study university in the implementation of interventions to enhance the quality of teaching as it strives to improve student access and success. The contribution to the literature would be an in-depth case study on institutional change in a well-resourced South African university as it responds to external and internal demands for change in the provision of teaching and learning.

Methodology
I will draw on four research methods:

- Documentary analysis of national and university policies and structures, including the use of secondary data to situate the single-site case study within the context nationally
- In depth interviews with project leaders, institutional managers at the university and national government officials
- Participant observation of committee and project meetings
- Evaluation of TDG projects

Research Ethics
Besides confidentiality and anonymity, my position within the case study university would raise ethical considerations for the proposed study. The proposal for the study would have to be rigorous enough to be cleared by the faculty and university Research Ethics Committees.

Commentary on revised sample proposal 4

This is now much better: more cohesive and convincing. However:

1. There is a shifting focus at the beginning between the *quality* of teaching and learning generally and changes in teaching and learning in line with the transformation agenda (that is, redressing the inequalities set in place by the apartheid regime). This potentially makes the research too broad. A supervisor's advice would probably be to concentrate on issues around the transformation agenda.

2. The research questions do not offer something that is of broader applicability. What is the significance of this research for **other** institutions or for national policy etc?

3. The discussion of Badat's work offers a clue to the answer to this question - the research offers an empirically-based detailed analysis of the structure versus agency debate in institutional change. This could have been highlighted in a new, final, research question. Similarly, the Teaching Development Grants as a policy instrument could have been contrasted with other policy instruments which will undoubtedly be operating within the case study university, comparing relative effectiveness, the reactions to them and so on. This would also give the study broader significance.

4. The contribution to the literature section describes the study but does not really say what the contribution is. It says:
"The contribution to the literature would be an in-depth case study on institutional change in a well-resourced South African university as it responds to external and internal demands for change in the provision of teaching and learning."

This descriptive but not explanatory sentence confirms the impression that there is a weakness in the proposal in terms of its answer to the "*so what?*" question.

5. There is an issue about whether the methods described fully align with the research questions. In particular, practice on the ground appears to be missing, unless this might happen in the evaluation of the TDG projects. How do lecturers and their students respond to the policies researched and how is practice actually changing in the classroom?

6. The final bullet point in the methodology section is not specific enough: how will that evaluation occur, what methods will be used?

7. The detail of samples, selection criteria and so on is missing from the methodology section. For bullet points are not enough to describe data collection methods, analysis approaches, sampling strategies etc. There is a gap in the proposal in terms of these details.

8. For a confirmation document (as opposed to an application for study, which this is) the literature would need to be more extensive.

Glossary

Academic register: A register is a particular tone and use of words that are appropriate to a given social setting. So academic register is one used in the context of writing academic books, articles or a doctorate. It is formal, tends to use Latinate words, uses compound nouns, passive voice and so on.

Action research: A cyclical process of collecting and analysing data, reflection and taking or amending action in order to bring about enhancement in practices and outcomes in the area being researched.

Advance organizer: "An advance organizer is information that is presented prior to learning and that can be used by the learner to organize and interpret new incoming information" (Mayer, 2007).

Cherry picking: In this context, being consistently selective about the data or literature used in order to substantiate an argument already formulated.

Conceptual closure: Deciding too early about the conclusions that can be derived from the data, and so ignoring evidence which contradicts those.

Discursive repertoires: Recurrently-used phrases, words, images or metaphors which situate the world in specific ways.

Elite policy study: A research project which studies top-level policy-makers or those who implement policy.

Empirical: Using primary data, collecting evidence from the world or observing it.

Empiricism: An approach to research which focuses on factual data without explicit or acknowledged use of theory, usually adopting a foundationalist position (see below).

Ethnography: A research approach which draws on multiple data sources to provide a detailed account of a cultural field.

Epistemology: Theories of knowledge and wh known.

Foundationalism: An ontological position which external reality exists independent from .... apprehension of it.

Grounded Theory: An approach to research which begins with data collection and from that process generates a series of concepts which have explanatory power. It is an inductive approach rather than the more usual hypothetico-deductive one. The latter begins with hypotheses and theory and tests them against data using a design which arises from the logic of the hypothesis.

Hypothetico-deductive tradition: An approach to research which involves establishing an hypothesis and then testing it against reality. Part of the scientific method.

Incommensurability: A situation in which theoretical positions are adopted which take such different ontological and epistemological standpoints that they are not comparable with each other, leaving no grounds for determining which is the most accurate.

Insider research: The study of social institutions by those who are actors in them. See Trowler (2012a) for more information on doing insider research.

Instrumentalism: Ideas guided by a desire for practical application, their value being measured by the success of the outcomes of that action.

Methods: In research, includes the specific techniques used to gather data or to analyse them.

Methodology: In research, refers to the set of principles and conventions which set out how research should be done and what it can achieve and therefore guides research planning.

Normative: Taking a committed stance about preferred present or future situations.

Ontology: Theory of the nature of 'reality', for example realist or social constructionist.

Operationalisation: The process of defining the elements of a concept in order to make its characteristics more capable of being researched or measured.

Prescriptive: Giving directions about what to do.

Policy trajectory study: A research project which follows a particular policy area from its inception through the various phases of implementation and finally collects data on the outcomes it has brought about, if any.

Realism: An ontological position which posits that an object reality exists which can be apprehended through research.

'So what?' question: The question which runs: "So what is the wider significance of this research to the academic community generally and/or to the economy, society or culture?"

Truth claims: In this context this refers to the claims made for the outcomes of the research in terms of how and where they can be applied and how robust they are.

References

(All websites last accessed 28.9.2015)

Arum, A. And Roksa, J. (2011) *Academically Adrift: Limited learning on college campuses.* Chicago: University of Chicago Press.

Astin, A. (2011) In 'Academically Adrift,' Data Don't Back Up Sweeping Claim. *The Chronicle of Higher Education,* February 14. Available at: http://chronicle.com/article/Academically-Adrift-a/126371/

Backhouse , J. P. (2009) *Doctoral Education in South Africa: Models, pedagogies and student experiences.* Johannesburg: University of Witwatersrand. https://www.academia.edu/820332/Doctoral_educatio n_in_South_Africa_Models_pedagogies_and_student_ex periences

Ball, S. J. (1995) Intellectuals or Technicians? The urgent role of theory in educational studies. *British Journal of Educational Studies,* 43, 255-271.

Bell, J. *Doing Your Research Project.* London: Open University Press.

Bensimon, E. M., Polkinghorne, D.E., Bauman, G. & Vallejo, E. (2004). Doing Research that Makes a Difference. *The Journal of Higher Education,* 75, 1, 104-126.

Coghlan, D and Brannick, T. (2010) *Doing Action Research in Your Own Organization.* (3rd edition). London: Sage.

Coleman, S. and von Hellermann, P. (2011) *Multi-Sited Ethnography: Problems and possibilities in the translocation of research methods.* London: Routledge.

Cooperrider, D. L. and Srivastva, S. *(1987)* Appreciative Inquiry in Organizational Life. *Research in Organizational Change and Development,* 1, 129-169.

Devault, M. L. (2006) What is Institutional Ethnography? *Social Problems,* 53, 3, 294-298.

Hammersley, M. (1993) On The Teacher As Researcher. In M. Hammersley (ed) *Educational Research: Current issues*. Buckingham: Open University Press.

Haraway, D. J. (1991) *Simians, Cyborgs and Women: The reinvention of nature*. New York: Routledge.

Hey, V. (2006) The Politics Of Performative Resignification: Translating Judith Butler's theoretical discourse and its potential for a sociology of education, *British Journal of Sociology of Education*, 27, 4, 439-457.

Koshy, V. (2009) *Action Research for Improving Educational Practice: A step-by-step guide*. London: Sage (second edition).

Mand, K. (2011) Researching Lives in Motion: Multi-Sited strategies in a transnational context. In S. Coleman and P. von Hellermann (2011) *Multi-Sited Ethnography: Problems and possibilities in the translocation of research methods*. London: Routledge.

Marcus, G. E. (2011) Multi-Sited Ethnography: Five or six things I know about it now. In S. Coleman and P. von Hellermann (2011) *Multi-Sited Ethnography: Problems and possibilities in the translocation of research methods*. London: Routledge.

Patton, Q. M. (1997) *Utilization-Focused Evaluation*. London: Sage. (Third edition).

Pawson, R. and Tilley, N. (1997) *Realistic Evaluation*. London: Sage.

Porter, S. (1993) Critical Realist Ethnography: The case of racism and professionalism in a medical setting. *Sociology*, 7, 4, 591-609.

Saunders, M., Trowler, P. and Bamber, V. (eds) (2011) *Reconceptualising Evaluation in Higher Education: The practice turn*. London: Open University Press.

Smith, D. E. (2005) *Institutional Ethnography: A sociology for people*. Lanham, MD: AltaMira.

Sprague, J. and Hayes, J. (2000) Self-Determination and Empowerment: A feminist standpoint analysis of talk about disability. *American Journal of Community Psychology*, 28, 5, 671-695.

Trowler, P. (2001) Captured By The Discourse? The socially constitutive power of new higher education discourse in the UK. *Organization*, 8, 2, 183-201.

Trowler, P. (2012) Wicked Issues in Situating Theory in Close Up Research. *Higher Education Research and Development.* 31, 3, 273-284.

****

More of Paul's Books for Doctoral Students

Trowler, P. (2014) *Frequently Asked Questions About Doctoral Research Into Higher Education.* E-book or physical book, available on Amazon.

Trowler, P. (2012) *Doctoral Research into Higher Education: Making theory work.* E-book or physical book, available on Amazon.

Trowler, P. (2012) *Writing Doctoral Project Proposals: Higher Education Research.* E-book or physical book, available on Amazon.

Trowler, P. (2012) *Doctoral Research into Higher Education: Thesis structure, content and completion.* E-book or physical book, available on Amazon.

Trowler, P. (2012) *Doing Insider Research in Universities: A short guide.* E-book or physical book, available on Amazon.

Trowler, P. (2012) *Higher Education Policy and Institutional Change.* E-book or physical book, available on Amazon. 2nd edition.

Trowler, P. (2014) *Supporting Online Learning: The case of "Policy and Change Processes in Higher Education" - A doctoral programme module.* Smashwords edition.

Praise for the first edition of this book

⭐⭐⭐⭐⭐ **Another little gem in this series!** 29 March 2013

Fabulous! An absolute must if you are starting a PhD journey. Concise and easily understood. Lots of excellent, practical tips that I, for one, have every intention of using in practice. I'm really glad I've read 3 in this series .... all three were read and my notes done in about a day or so .... so I have a good grounding for starting my work once ethical approval has been granted. If you read no other 'how to' books on PhD... read these. In my view, total 'must haves'!

another little gem in this series!

⭐⭐⭐⭐⭐ **Very useful – recommended.** 28 August 2013

I'm new to doctoral study and needed a bit of a boost to my confidence and this has helped a lot. Paul Trowler writes in a very easy style for which I am grateful. He writes very clearly, in plain English and I look forward to referencing his text in my up-coming assignment! It is also a short text and so I did not feel at all hard-done-to reading it whilst on holiday, on the beach!

⭐⭐⭐⭐⭐ **Highly recommended if you don't know how to submit a proposal.** 25 May 2015

Very helpful. I had little idea of how to structure a proposal until I read this. It has been emphasised to me by my university that the proposal should be completed independently of the university: basically I'm on my own until when or if the proposal is accepted.

This book made me feel a little less on my own and provided some sound advice. I'm now much more confident in what I need to do to submit a proposal.

★★★★★ **Compact and elaborate.** 17 Jan. 2015

I bought Writing Doctoral Project... as a gift for my daughter and I read the whole book in less than one hour. It's a compact book with complete guidance on your way to a successful doctoral project. I recommend this book to those intending to embark on a project of their own.

★★★★★ **Very useful if you intend to write up your PhD.**16 February 2015

Gives you understanding on how to write an PhD proposal with guidance and structure. Also refers to paradigms with explanation.Paul's website is at www.paul-trowler.weebly.com

---

END OF THE BOOK